Insect Repellents:

10 Homemade Organic Non-Toxic Mosquito and Ant Repellent

Table of content

Introduction

To begin, this book serves as a manual for mosquito and ant repellents. Since the bugs including mosquitoes, midges and ticks have unmistakable loathsome effects on an individual's life, from now on, there must be such antagonistic to authorities which can exhaust such bugs. Shockingly, the counter specialists made by the creators in colossal affiliations fuse the utilization of chemicals; in this manner it is urged to make the counter bugs fluids at home. These threatening to administrators will give thriving and security from the alarming little animals and besides the chemicals. The oils and herbs utilized as a bit of sales to control these repulsive bugs are joined as well.

Further, certain formulas to make these against creepy crawlies are given. Firstly, the reliable formulas to rebuke mosquitoes are consolidated here. Moreover, homemade repellents are preferred over the commercial repellents because they are skin- friendly and efficient. Thirdly, conditions to keep ticks far from oneself are besides included. Fourthly, trademark segments for appalling minimal creature against operators are set here to clarify the ambiguities. Finally, outside threatening to administrators for bugs are clarified in this book. Curiously, the majority of the ruinous effects of the over the top use of these threatening to administrators are cleared up her. This book, in this way, gives a profound understanding about those strategies utilized as a part of request to keep mosquitoes, creepy crawlies, ants and comparable bugs away. Besides, the greater part of the medicine and creams that can be utilized after creepy crawlies nibble are additionally included here. Accordingly, this book is a finished bundle to help the peruser in disposing of creepy crawlies from his/her life.

Also, a huge finding out about those herbs and oils is given which can be utilized to the making of these threatening to masters at home. Hence, this book will give data which one have to know with a specific completed target to keep the bugs including midges, mosquitoes and ticks away.

Chapter 1 – Tips to Keep Mosquitos and Ants Away from Your House

Nobody needs their home to be encompassed by mosquitoes and ants. Regardless of their little size, they can be hazardous. They are in charge of various sorts of ailments including fever and dengue. However, how might you rebuff them without hurting the environment and without showing your family to any conceivably ruinous chemicals, is the real issue. In order to find the answer to your questions, continue reading. Some of the tips to keep these creepy insects away are as follows:

- **Use peppermint:**

    Arachnids detest peppermint and it is not destructive to your wellbeing too. A basic way to deal with keep creepy crawlies far from assaulting your space is to fill a sprinkle bottle with peppermint imperative oil and water, and a while later shower it around your home. Furthermore, this will enhance the look of your home.

    Peppermint oil is also used in order to keep large variety of bugs out of your home. Moreover, it possesses numerous other important features as well.

- **Make a clean environment:**

    The least costly and most common way to deal with mosquitoes and other bugs is extremely simple. What you need to do is to just keep your environment clean. Keeping your home flawless, perfect and free of dust or systems is the best way to deal with keep 8-legged creature from moving in. Ordinary vacuuming, cleaning, and mopping will keep most of the dreadful little animals away from your sight.

- **Utilization of vinegar:**

White vinegar has around five trillion uses around the house and spurning 8-legged creature is one of them. Shocking creepy crawlies with vinegar is much like spurning them with peppermint oil, in that you fill a sprinkle bottle with vinegar and water, and shower every one of the breaks and gap around your home.

- **Obstruct the entrance:**

A mind blowing way to deal with keep creepy crawlies out of your home is to never give them access regardless. Guarantee the outside of your home is free from leaves, grass clippings, stacks of wood, or whatever different notorious 8-legged creature joints. You can similarly check all gateway openings and windowsills to guarantee there is no space for frightening little creatures to get in that way, and apply caulk when required.

- **Use citrus peels:**

It is a fundamental discovering that mosquitoes and ants hate all things citrus. Rubbing citrus peels on regions where bugs are, aversion baseboards, windowsills and bookshelves, is a wonderful way to deal with keep them from coming around. Despite using lemon scented furniture sparkle can push dreadful little creatures away.

- **Utilization of cedar to remove insects:**

Cedar can be an inconceivable prevention for mosquitoes and ants. You can use cedar mulch outside around the fringe of your home to endeavor to keep 8-legged creature from relentlessly getting inside. In case you have cedar holder then use them in your storage space. Moreover, use cedar squares or shavings inside closets, coordinators or drawers can make them consider hanging out in there too.

- **Use of chestnuts:**

They have been known for obstructing insects, so setting some of them in your windows gaps or even along your baseboards can keep bugs from hanging out there. Various people in like manner trust that the same thing ought to be conceivable with an Osage orange. In order to keep the mosquitoes away, place chestnuts in the house. In addition to them, you can also put hedge apples in the house. However, you must not keep them for too long. If they are spoiled then you must get rid of them.

- **Use tobacco:**

It sounds different, yet creepy crawlies loathe tobacco basically as much as they hate lemons and chestnuts. You can sprinkle little bits of tobacco where ants are troublesome, or you can retain tobacco water and a short time later sprinkle the mix all around. Regardless, tobacco is really excessive these days, so you can likely find a more sensible fix for holding creepy crawlies under control.

- **Normal mosquito repellents:**

You can make your own specific shower and sprinkle it in the areas where ants and mosquitoes are found. For instance, the washroom and other drenched extents in your home. Moreover, spray it in the garden area or even along windows and portals so that the insects could not enter your house. To make this mixture, take some squeezed apple vinegar, a teaspoon of oil, some pepper and a teaspoon of cleanser. Put it in a splashing bottle and spray on the insects. In order to increase the efficiency, you can shower it again.

- **Borax:**

Borax is most by and large used to keep ants out, in any case it rebuffs creepy crawlies too in light of the way that it butchers them if they get into it. Basically sprinkle this on the entry areas of the ants and then catch them up. Similarly, you can put this between your window and whirlwind windows and along the edges of your passages. Borax powder is found easily on shops and grocery stores. Once you have placed the borax powder on the attacked area, it will be safe for a few hours.

Chapter 2 – Overview of Commercial Insect Repellents

In order to repel multiple kinds of insects, various repellent are made commercially. Some of them are used to repel and kill mosquitoes or any specific insect, whereas some of them are used for all kinds of insects. These repellents hold great importance in the commercial market; however, they possess some chemicals which are harmful to human health and skin. Therefore, they must not be used. In addition, when these repellents are applied on the soil, they can also hamper the fertility of soil; thus, causing a lot of trouble for the user. In order to eradicate this issue, some people prefer using the homemade repellents.

Numerous chemical agents have been used in the past to repel the insects. Moreover, researches are always being conducted to test new chemicals. Some of the chemicals are always utilized to make a repellent; some of them are as follows:

- Picardin

- Permethrin

- DEET

- IR3535

All of these chemicals have different properties. However, they possess side effects as well, which drags down their usefulness.

1. **DEET:**

   Insect anti-agents containing DEET are being utilized for over 50 years. They possess the ability to repulse mosquitoes, ants and other insects. They are considered as the gold standard in the insect repellents.

2. **Picaridin:**

   Picaridin is generally as powerful as DEET since it is equally efficient. On the brighter side, it can cause lesser itching and irritation.

3. **Oil of Lemon Eucalyptus:** Oil of Lemon Eucalyptus, plant-based anti-agents, is additionally enrolled as anti-agents by the EPA. Some examines directed in the US tried the viability of this oil as bug repellent. Results demonstrated that it gave insurance simply like anti-agents with low convergences of DEET.

4. **Permethrin:**

   Permethrin is another anti-agent that is planned for application on apparel and hardware.

Therefore, it can be deduced that there are huge number of items that can be connected on skin to keep the creepy crawly nibbles and related risks. Each item or synthetic has its own particular favorable circumstances and drawbacks.

Having the best information about such creepy crawly repellent items is the fundamental key to comprehend the working and diverse parts of bug repellants. The requirement for utilizing such items shifts as indicated by geographic territories. It is urgent to utilize mosquito anti-agents in a territory of unreasonable mosquitoes to evade jungle fever, and creepy crawly anti-agents are the instruments to accomplish it.

Chapter 3 – Recipes for Homemade Mosquito Repellents

Since the disclosure of a tropical insects, perceived as a conveyor of deadly malaria by Sir Ronald Russ, people have been concentrating on mosquitoes. It is an impeccable opportunity to get comfortable with your neighborhood mosquitoes and lay some cautious game-plans about how to keep mosquitoes away. A singular nibble from a tainted mosquito can transmit the sickness to a human, stallion or flying creature. A really solid immunization is accessible for steeds; given in two estimations, it gives insurance after around two months. For people and pet flying creatures, minimizing preamble to mosquitoes is the most ideal approach to maintain a strategic distance from potential debasement.

Since the bugs including mosquitoes, ants and ticks have specific damaging impacts on an individual's life; thusly, there must be such against powers which can clear such crawling startling little animals. Shockingly, the counter geniuses made by the makers in gigantic affiliations join the usage of chemicals. Henceforth, it is requested that make mosquito and ants repellents at home. These disagreeable to managers will give achievement and security from the frightening little creatures furthermore the chemicals.

In addition, it is altogether easy to make one's own particular standard mosquito repellent. One can control unquestionably what goes into the thing so you would not have to push over any undesirable chemicals. There are a couple of excellent definitions you can make for your ordinary mosquito repellent. On the contrary, the oils do not blend with water, so one should add them to different oils or to liquor. It's essential to utilize an oil or liquor that is legitimate for the skin. Additionally, do not continue running over the edge with the noteworthy oils. The oils are strong and could accomplish skin irritation or another response in the event that you utilize excessively. In any case, a pregnant woman must not utilize any mosquito repellent, neither basic nor for the most part, until after one has gotten it cleared by the expert.

The general formula for mosquitoes repellent incorporates vital and carrier oils.

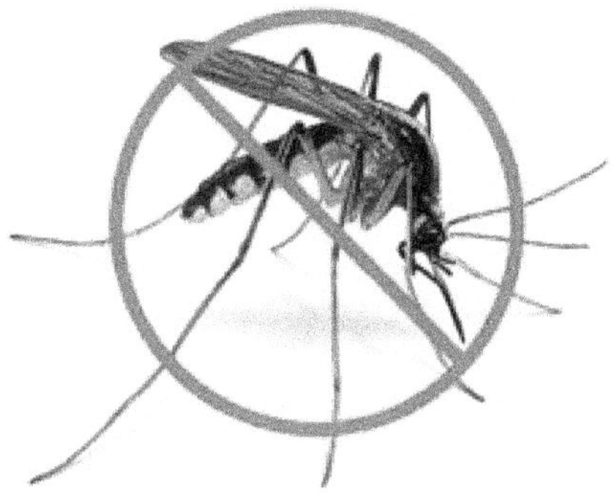

1. **Essential oils:**

   A bit of the essential oils that come well against the mosquitoes are according to the accompanying:

   i.   Lemon Eucalyptus Oil.

   ii.   Cinnamon Oil.

   iii.   Castor Oil.

   iv.   Citronella Oil.

2. **Carrier Oils:**

Two or three the secured transporter oils that are appropriate for mosquito against operators are according to the accompanying:

i.   Sunflower Oil.

ii.   Olive oil.

iii.   Witch Hazel.

3. Moreover, alcohol can be used in making mosquito repellents. Vodka is the common kind of alcohol used to serve the purpose.

General Recipe of Mosquito Repellent:

Firstly, blend the key oil with the carrier oil. Rub or sprinkle the mosquito repellent onto the skin or garments. In any case, manage not to utilize the counter operators on the tricky regions of one's body e.g. eyes. Moreover, one needs to apply this mixture each time after around a hour or in the wake of swimming or work out. Unused hostile to specialists must be secured in a dull compartment, far from warmth or daylight.

Taking after are a part of the recipes for consistent mosquito against operators used as a rule:

Lemon Eucalyptus Mosquito Repellent:

Ingredients:

Following are the required ingredients:

i.   Witch hazel.

ii.   Lemon eucalyptus oil.

iii.   Sunflower oil.

Procedure:

Following is the procedure for this recipe

i.   Combine all things in such manner that 1 part of lemon eucalyptus oil with each ten segments of the sunflower or witch hazel.

ii.   Mix the mix well.

iii.   Put the liquid or sprinkle it on your skin.

Lavender Vanilla Repellent:

Ingredients:

Given below are the ingredients:

i.   Lemon juice- Three to four tablespoons.

ii.   Vanilla concentrate- Three to four tablespoon.

iii.   Lavender crucial oil- Fifteen drops.

iv.   Distilled water.

Procedure:

i.   Following procedure must be used to make the recipe:

ii.   Mix the prescribed measures of lemon juice, vanilla concentrate and lavender essential oil into a sprinkle container.

iii.   After merging them, incorporate refined water into them.

iv.   Shake the fixings together.

v.   Spray on the pined for part or articles of clothing.

Clove and Baby Oil Repellent:

Ingredients:

The fixings used for this equation are:

i.   Cloves- 3.5 oz.

ii.   Alcohol- 16 oz.

iii.   Baby oil- 3.5 oz.

Method:

Following procedure must be adopted:

i.   Put the cloves in alcohol and marinate them for four days

ii.   However, keep blending the mix two times every day.

iii.   Afterwards, shake them well and shower on the hungered for spot.

Cinnamon oil and citronella:

Ingredients:

The ingredients used for this formula are:

i.   Castor oil- Two oz.

ii.   Cinnamon oil- 5 drops.

iii.   Eucalyptus oil- 15 drops

iv.   Sunflower oil- Six oz.

v.   Citronella- Fifteen drops.

Method:

Following method is used to make this recipe:

i.   Mix most of the fixings in a holder.

ii.   Shake the mix well to avoid any development.

iii.   Spray for better results.

Chapter 4 – Recipe for Homemade Ant Repellents

Bugs that fly are adequately startling, however flying ants might be altogether scarier. Ants are commonly seen inching on the ground, so it's staggering when ants with wings start murmuring around. Winged ants end up being impressively all the all the more driving when they swarm in the midst of mating periods, gathering at specific purposes of enthusiasm for a behavior called slope topping.

These creepy crawlies in all probability create more fear, hating, and bother than any others found in the home. For cockroaches particularly these reactions are legitimized, since they do transmit sickness and trigger hypersensitivities and asthma. Ants and flies, also, can corrupt support.

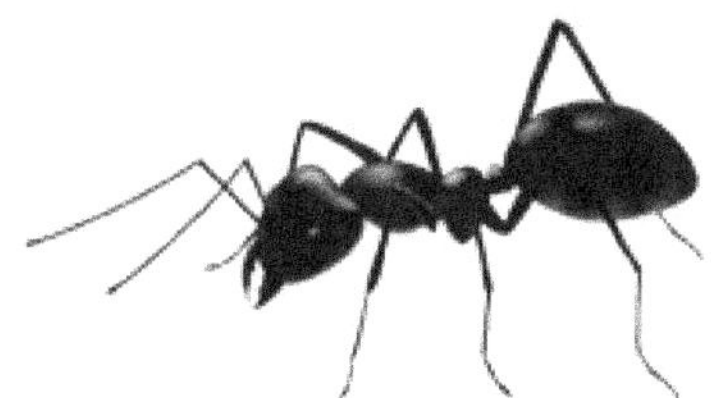

Our strength for creatures with six or more legs in our homes is low, and because of the compelling sentiments they mix in us, we are capable to reach thusly for the vaporized bug sprinkle. In light of present circumstances, it's straightforward that you do not have to get close to the bugs, and you have the satisfaction of seeing them kick the container. In any case, you must hold up.

Pesticides used inside will store on surfaces, for instance, kitchen counters, adolescents' toys, and floor covers where kids play. Children can ingest the pesticide after some time through hand-to-mouth contract. Likewise, since showering doesn't address the explanation behind the issue, the aggravations frequently will return. Taking after are a portion of the focuses that must be taken after to maintain a strategic distance from the ants and different creepy crawlies:

- One must keep vegetation concealing the house to a base. This diminishes bugs harboring areas and improved wind stream including the house. Engineering with tallish vegetation with an upper tree shade is charming over low, thick vegetation in midge inclined ranges as it permits an endlessly improved wind stream close ground level.

- On the distant chance that midges are an issue entering through fly screens, stop the insignificant cross portion areas. Screens can in like way be sprinkled with the fresher low hurtful surface showers containing manufactured pyrethroids to stay away from midge entering.

- Bug getting gadgets utilizing ultra violet light as the attractant are by and large pointless for decreasing biting midge numbers in common yards. Traps utilizing carbon dioxide as an attractant must be particularly represented and worked moreover intentionally put to have any conceivable obliging impact.

- Customized pyrethroid limit sprinkles, put around the vegetation area and outside the dividers may astonishingly decrease midge grown-up numbers around treated premises for a long time.

- It is no doubt midge will enter abodes the leeward or guaranteed side of the living game plan. Close leeward windows or keep openings little when midges are an issue.

- As mosquitoes always look to hunt down blood suppers when a moderate breeze is blowing, housetop fans or other air course gadgets that production wind stream inside the residence in like way diminish gnawing midge unsettling impact inside.

- Moreover, some of the useful mosquito repellent oils are as below:

    i.   Citronella.

    ii.   Bergamot.

    iii.   Tea tree.

    iv.   Rose geranium.

    v.   Lemon.

    vi.   Peppermint.

    vii.   Cypress.

    viii. Eucalyptus.

Homemade Repellents:

In any case, ant's repellents use differing key oils like:

    i. Lavender.

    ii. Lemon.

    iii. Eucalyptus.

Furthermore, society results with these in light of current circumstances waver paying little heed to the way that the standard purpose of interest is that they are altogether less inclined to understand a response or any entire arrangement hurt.

A part of the locally developed hostile to operators is according to the accompanying:

Vinegar and oil:

Ingredients:

Following are the ingredients:

i.   Squeezed apple vinegar- One tablespoon.

ii.   Two tablespoon of the following oils:

    a. Lavender.

    b. Mint.

    c. Rosemary.

    d. Thyme.

Method:

Taking after technique must be gotten for the productive making of this equation:

i.   Place vinegar and dried herbs into a noteworthy glass compartment.

ii.   Seal undauntedly and store on counter or place you will see it reliably. Shake well every day for 2-3 weeks.

iii.   Following 2-3 weeks, strain the herbs out and store in sprinkle compartments or tincture bottles, ideally in cooler.

iv.   To use on skin, weaken to half with water in a sprinkle holder and use as required.

v.   Use whenever you want to get rid of ants.

Garlic Mosquito Repellent

Ingredients:

Following are the ingredients:

i.   Lime juice.

ii.   Mineral oil.

iii.   Finely minced garlic.

Method:

Following strategy must be gotten for the successful making of this recipe:

i.   Mince a few cloves of garlic.

ii.   Then cover them with some mineral oil.

iii.   Permit it to sit for practically 24 hours.

iv.   Take a teaspoon of oil and blend it well with some water close by one teaspoon of fresh lime juice.

v.   Strain through a cheesecloth in the event that any air pockets are accessible then fill a sprinkle bottle.

vi.   Shake whenever required.

Cedar wood and rosemary:

Ingredients:

Following are the required ingredients:

i.   Lemon eucalyptus oil- fifty drops.

ii.   Cedar wood oil- fifteen drops.

iii.   Lavender oil- fifteen drops.

iv.   Rosemary- Fifteen drops.

Method:

Following method must be used:

i.   To begin, add transporter fluids to little shower bottle.

ii.   Afterwards, include the vital oils.

iii.   Shake well before you use.

iv.   Moreover, typical bug repellent should be reapplied typically for most noticeable practicality.

Additionally, you must bear in mind the following precautions while using any of these recipes:

- While using pivotal oils, ladies who are pregnant or nursing ought to meet a doctor before utilizing.

- Great consideration ought to be utilized while utilizing vital oils on enthusiastic young people.

- Continuously play out a patch test to check for an unfavorably feeble response before utilizing basic oil shockingly.

- Continuously name hand made things well.

- Dull shaded compartments work best for things containing basic oils.

- Store in a cool, dry spot when not utilizing.

Chapter 5 – Natural Repellents for Garden Bugs

The insect anti-agents are substances associated on to the surfaces, skin or articles of clothing to keep bugs from landing or bouncing on them. The commercial repellents are more capable and tough than homemade when it comes to effect. These against specialists foresee and control the scene of creepy crawlies borne diseases like intestinal disorder, dengue fever et cetera. Bugs, for instance, bug, fly, mosquito and tick are the customary vectors for passing on these diseases. Some usually used frightening little animal hostile to operators are DEET, neem oil, essential oil of lemon eucalyptus, citronella oil, and permethrin.

Starting late, the usage of basic bug against specialists has wound up acclaimed. Herbs and diverse plants are used as amazing standard answers for keep away the bugs. Here are a few consistent responses to the inquiries regarding repelling the bugs. The harming impacts of bugs change dependent upon their region and nature. Notwithstanding, a couple general groupings of malevolent impacts of bugs are pervasive and happen with a mix of bugs. These impacts unite taking after huge issues:

i. Hinder Plant Growth:

Several sorts of frightening little creatures really impact the progression and change of new and creating plants. They cut the delicate tissues and suck out the juices. Unsettling influences Bug nibble for the most part have a couple appalling impacts. Some of them consolidate intensification and other perilous ailments. The less bona fide impact is the central worsening; swelling and torment that every so often start after get snacked by particular frightening little animals. Case in point, mosquitoes, honey bees and a few frightening little animals can achieve dangerous disorders going from intestinal ailment to dengue. Their eats can find the opportunity to be chafed, and the regions of the nibble may persuade the chance to be red and swollen from time to time.

ii. Illness:

The more true blue side of horrendous little animal eats is the ailment that can understand persuading cases. Unsafe frightening little animals, for case, the dull dowager and cocoa contemplative person can understand affirmed contamination, skin surrenders and despite going in phenomenal occasions. Certain ticks are praised bearers of the genuine Lyme illness or Rocky Mountain spotted fever, which can accomplish true blue flourishing issues for individuals.

iii. Ecological Concerns:

A ruinous impact made by bugs is the utilization of pesticides and other designed controls to keep them from harming yields and gardens. Different fields are showered with pesticides always. These pesticides can sting little creatures and even individuals who are routinely displayed to the chemicals in them. Nourishment creators are at times analyzed for liberal utilization of pesticides also. Natural social affairs screen utilization of pesticides and try to influence diverse contrasting options to controlling risky impacts startling little creatures have on fields and plant change.

The motivating news is that there are some universal bug executioners that can continue unnerving little animals off you, your children, your pets, and your yard nursery. Along these lines, a segment of the methodologies to spurn dreadful little creatures are according to the accompanying:

Oil of lemon eucalyptus:

This consistent oil, which begins from the lemon eucalyptus tree, is embraced as a substitute to DEET. It appears to work enormously well. Regardless, heartbreakingly that it has not picked up the thought it merits. A couple considers have discovered this standard bug repellent as productive as DEET in spurning frightening little creatures. It might in like way limit amazingly against ticks. Oil of lemon eucalyptus might be damaging if ingested in high entireties. As indicated by the CDC it ought not to be utilized on children under 3.

Researchers have endeavored different other guaranteed general bug unfriendly to administrators which fuses many:

i. Citronella.

ii. Peppermint oil.

Oil and vegetable glycerin:

Remembering the deciding objective to fight away the dreadful little animals make this shower. With the help of this sprinkle, one can control an extensive variety of frightening little animals

Ingredients:

- Essential oils, these oils might be one of the going with:

i. Clove oil.

ii. Eucalyptus oil.

iii. Citronella oil.

iv. Mint.

v. Rosemary oil.

vi. Lavender oil.

vii. Lemongrass oil.

viii. Cedar oil.

ix. Tee oil.

- Vegetable glycerin.

- Common Witch Hazel.

- Natively assembled Bug Spray.

- Refined or frothed Water.

Method:

i. Fill shower bottle 1/2 full with refined or frothed water.

ii. Add witch hazel to fill in every practical sense to the top.

iii. Then, include 1/2 teaspoon vegetable glycerin if utilizing.

iv. Include 30-50 drops of critical oils to wanted smell. The more oils you utilize, the more grounded the sprinkle will be.

Herbal Bug Spray:

Ingredients:

To make a profitable home developed bug shower, taking after fixings must be used:

- Refined water

- Witch hazel or

- Rubbing liquor

- Dried herbs, taking after dried herbs can be used:

    i. Peppermint.

    ii. Spearmint.

    iii. Citronella.

    iv. Lemon grass.

    v. Catnip.

    vi. Lavender.

Method:

i. Bubble some water and consolidate three to four tablespoon of dried herbs out of those which are recorded above and blend them.

ii. However, it is proposed to utilize one tablespoon each of peppermint, spearmint, catnip and lavender.

iii. Furthermore, fling in a couple dried cloves.

iv. Blend well, cover and let the mix cool. Besides, covering is fundamental to keep the abnormal oils in

v. Strain herbs out and blend water with some witch hazel or rubbing liquor. Store in a sprinkle bottle in a cool spot (ice chest is extraordinary in light of the way that then it is normal and cool).

vi. Use as required.

vii. Special reward: it smells awesome and is remarkably reestablishing to the skin.

Neem oil repellent:

Neem oil is used for multiple healthy purposes. One of the many benefits of neem oil is to repel insects and bugs. Given below is the recipe to make neem oil repellent.

Ingredients:

Following ingredients are used to make neem oil repellent:

i. Refine water- 1 liter.

ii. Neem oil- five bottles.

iii. Liquid hand wash- 2 bottles.

Method:

The method used to make a neem oil repellent is as follows:

i. To begin, combine water, neem oil and the liquid hand wash in a beaker.

ii. Afterwards, shake the mixture to combine them.

iii. Now put the solution in a bottle to splash.

iv. Spray on the bugs and see the results.

Conclusion

To put more or less, this book is a manual for the outside and indoor agents that will keep the mosquitoes, ants, and in addition different bugs away. Since these bugs have diverse terrible impacts on an individual's life, thusly, there must be repellents which can oust such crawling bugs. Shockingly, the counter operators made by the makers in monstrous associations incorporate the usage of chemicals. Therefore it is urged to make the bug repellent liquids at home. These hostile to operators will give prosperity and security from the bugs and likewise the chemicals. The oils and herbs used as a piece of solicitation to control these pernicious bugs are joined moreover.

Furthermore, some of the recipes to make these amazing repellents are included in this book. Moreover, most of the experiences concerning the measures of these hostile to operators are incorporated here. Firstly, the basic recipes to shock mosquitoes are incorporated here. Moreover, locally built hostile to operators for midges are furthermore clarified in here. Fourthly, the major components for bugs repellent are put here to clear up the ambiguities. All in all, outside hostile to operators for bugs are cleared up in this book. Inquisitively, most of the dangerous impacts of the over the top use of these against operators are elucidated her.

Plus, a significant comprehension about those herbs and oils is given which can be used to the generation of these hostile to operators at home. Thusly, this book is an amazing guide about home-made repellents.

FREE Bonus Reminder

If you have not grabbed it yet, please go ahead and download your special bonus report *"DIY Projects. 13 Useful & Easy To Make DIY Projects To Save Money & Improve Your Home!"*

Simply Click the Button Below

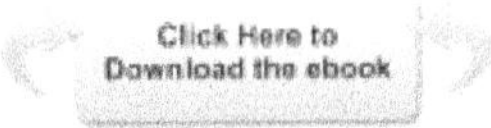

OR Go to This Page

http://healthylivingpeople.com/free/

BONUS #2: More Free & Discounted Books

Do you want to receive more Free & Discounted Books?

We have a mailing list where we send out our new Books when they go free or with a discount on Kindle. Click on the link below to sign up for Free & Discount Book Promotions.

=> Sign Up for Free & Discount Book Promotions <=

OR Go to this URL

www.ingramcontent.com/pod-product-compliance
Lightning Source LLC
Chambersburg PA
CBHW050803240726
48654CB00008B/618